RULES & PROCEDURES

A First Step Toward School Civility

BY
Dr. Philip Fitch Vincent

RULES & PROCEDURES

A FIRST STEP TOWARD SCHOOL CIVILITY

by Dr. Philip Fitch Vincent

Produced and published by

CHARACTER DEVELOPMENT GROUP

Phone (919) 967–2110, fax (919) 967–2139

E-mail respect96@aol.com

Cover design by Paul Turley

Book design by Sandy Nordman Design

Text editing by Trisha Rosemoon, Amy Barefoot, and Ginny Turner
Typeproofing—Lisa Brumback

ISBN 0-9653163-1-9 $14.00

Contents

"What the best and wisest parent wants for his own child, that must the community want for all of its children. Any other ideal for our schools is narrow and unlovely, acted upon, it destroys our democracy."

John Dewey, School and Society, 1910

Preface

RULES AND PROCEDURES: The First Step Toward School Civility is the first book in a five-book series utilizing the "Hub and Spokes" of character education. Rules and procedures represent the hub and are critical to the implementation of the other spokes of character education. Therefore it was the logical first choice. The other spokes will be featured in books over the next several years.

Each of these books will be written by experts in their field and will provide background and insights in assisting schools and school districts to develop solid approaches to character education. I look forward to continuing dialogue with these authors as I struggle to enhance my own understanding of solid character-education practices.

This book would not have been possible without the insights of individuals such as Kevin Ryan, Tom Lickona, Henry Huffman and William Damon. The clarity of your writing illuminates difficult issues and forces us, who aspire to write a few words, to be clear and concise in our attempts. Although I will credit you when I am successful, I will not hold you responsible for my failures.

I am particularly grateful for my friendship with David Wangaard from the School for Ethical Education in Bridgeport, Connecticut. David's insights in this text cannot be overestimated. The hours we have spent in discussions have greatly enhanced my knowledge of character education and, more importantly, have contributed to a friendship which continues to grow.

I am grateful for the fresh ideas of practitioners around the country. Whether I am working in North Carolina, Texas, Oregon, Connecticut or any of my other destinations, excellent educators challenge me in my assumptions and force me to think and re-think my assertions. You teach me far more than I ever teach you.

Thanks to Dixon, Amy, and Lisa at Character Development Group, who man the phones and assist countless people around the country in their character education efforts.

Finally I thank my wife, Cynthia and daughter Mary Kathryn. I am only able to continue to travel because of your support and constant love.

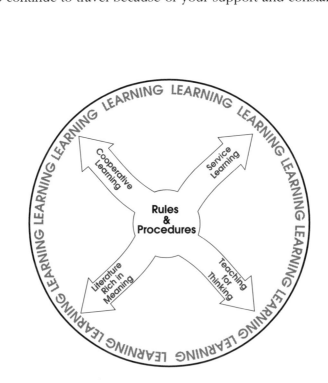

Introduction

The core problem facing our schools is a moral one. All the other problems derive from it. Hence, all the various attempts at school reform are unlikely to succeed unless character education is put at the top of the agenda. If students don't learn self discipline and respect for others, they will continue to exploit each other sexually no matter how many health clinics and condom distribution plans are created. If they don't learn habits of courage and justice, curriculums designed to improve their self-esteem won't stop the epidemic of extortion, bullying, and violence; neither will courses designed to make them more sensitive to diversity....If they don't acquire intellectual virtues such as commitment to learning, objectivity, respect for the truth, and humility in the face of facts, then critical-thinking strategies will only amount to one more gimmick in the curriculum.

William Kilpatrick
Why Johnny Can't Tell Right From Wrong

William Kilpatrick's analysis of school reform needing character education at the top of its agenda has never been more relevant as we approach the twenty-first century. This moral problem facing our schools that he alludes to is one that has recuperative potential. Remedying this problem calls for the provision of a moral environment in schools for all students. Such an environment requires structure bounded by fairness. This environment emphasizes a love of learning balanced with a love of good action which leads to civility. James Kauffman and Harold Burbach (1997) recognize the importance of basic civilities:

> "At a minimum, the kind of social climate we envision is one in which everyone, teachers and students alike, treats others with consideration and respect and in which mannerly behavior and small courtesies are the norm. More optimistically, we believe that a classroom where civility holds sway is one that is well on its way to facilitating classroom cooperation, responsible self-governance, and democratic living." (p. 322)

This type of environment prompts a school to operate as a good community, thus enabling students to function within the dynamics of a good community. Educators must recognize the importance of modeling good habits so students can develop such behaviors themselves. If we insist that students be fair and honest, we must be fair and honest. If we desire that students are caring, we must be caring. If we want students to be polite, we must be polite.

Modeling is necessary but, alone, it is not enough to insure that a moral climate exists in a school. Students need time to work together, to reflect and discuss ideas that are the natural result of good readings, and to serve others in the school and community. Students also need order and structure. Developing guidelines via rules and procedures help insure a good and just community.

It is elemental that good parents and teachers spend time on establishing such productive rules and procedures. Children exposed to these helpful guidelines, which nurture habits of respect, responsibility, perseverance, etc., are more likely to be successful in school and in life than those who are unexposed.

As we examine *rules* and *procedures* and construct a corroborative platform on which to begin our discussion, let us define these terms in a workable context.

Webster's dictionary defines a **rule** as: *an authoritative regulation for action, conduct, method, procedure, arrangement, etc. {the rules of the school}.* **Procedure** is defined as: *the act, method, or manner of proceeding in some process or course of action; esp., the sequence of steps to be followed 2. a particular course of action or way of doing something.*

We can infer, then, that rules set the standard that conduct tries to meet. Procedures tell us what to do to meet the objectives of the rule(s). The practice of procedures leads to a following of the rules and the subsequent development of good habits of action. Developing good character traits, as Aristotle has noted, is habitual. The failure to cultivate good habits such as respect, punctuality, courtesy and responsibility dooms a child to actions based on impulses without the character needed to develop into a good citizen.

Luckily, the majority of students recognize the importance of observing rules and procedures. They understand that the failure to follow society's basic rules and procedures results in behavior which is counterproductive to positive living and learning.

However, there is ample evidence that far too many students today are rejecting following rules and practicing appropriate procedures. Many are favoring actions based on their individual desires without regard to the potential outcomes. We need only talk with educators to learn that the overall behavior of students in schools has seriously deteriorated from even twenty years ago. In general, students are exhibiting less respect for teachers and for their peers. They are more prone to break or disregard rules and accepted norms of behavior at school and within the community.

The Josephson Institute's 1996 study of 6,000 high school students noted that 87 percent of them believed that, on a practical basis, honesty is the best policy. (One can only wonder what the other 13 percent believe!) Based on other responses within the survey, however, it is clear this statement concerning the importance of honesty is not carrying over to other behaviors.

- Two-thirds of the students (65 percent) admitted they had cheated on an exam in the previous year and about half, or 47 percent, said they had done so more than once.
- Forty-two percent of high school male respondents and 31 percent of high school females said they had stolen something from a store within the previous 12 months.
- More than half the high school male respondents (55 percent) and one-third of the females (36 percent) said it is sometimes justified to respond to an insult or verbal abuse with physical force.

William Bennett, in *The Index of Leading Cultural Indicators: Facts and Figures on the State of American Society* (1994), noted some chilling trends of students in or near schools.

- About 3 million thefts and violent crimes occur on or near a school campus each year, representing nearly 16,000 incidents per day.
- Twenty percent of high school students now carry a firearm, knife, razor, club, or some other weapon on a regular basis.

These statistics raise the all important question: *Why is this occurring?* Children can't be totally accountable for these trends. They have learned these behaviors from someone; they aren't born with such negative tendencies. Children are born with certain dispositions which can be developed into moral behavior (more about this will follow in Chapter 2). However, if they are left without a guide—without a moral compass—they may choose a more harmful and potentially destructive path. Children, for the most part, act based on what is expected of them. They learn by observation and by instruction. They learn by the development of good and bad habits.

Despite the preceding statistics, the majority of our students have been taught to be civil and caring toward others and practice this most of the time. They are on the path to good citizenship. However, simply striving for a majority is not adequate. All of our students deserve the opportunity to develop good habits to assist them throughout their lives. In helping them develop their character —to *know the good, love the good and do the good*—we as parents and educators are giving them tools to navigate through their lives. This book will focus on how rules and procedures can facilitate this process.

RULES & PROCEDURES

1

RULES AND PROCEDURES GENERATE A WINNING CLIMATE IN SCHOOLS

Life is regulated by rules and procedures. An individual who wants a college degree agrees to follow the rules and procedures of the university in order to obtain the degree. For example, a rule governing when a class can be dropped without penalty of grade is one the college student might encounter. Actually dropping the class reflects the procedure necessary to complete the prescribed drop/add process. The student must also adhere to requirements for the number of credit hours required to graduate.

Likewise, public and private schools have rules which describe how students and educators should act. Following rules helps create a civil environment within which teachers and students can operate. Such guidelines help create discipline and good habits. Yet not every child or adult will follow rules compliantly. Some lack a recognition of the implicit value of rules. Others follow rules only because they are concerned about the consequences if they don't.

The issue of punctuality illustrates why having a tardy rule for students and teachers encourages timely attendance. Many will comply because they recognize that, if people are habitually late, no serious instruction can occur. Others will follow the tardy rule because of the potential consequences that result from being tardy to class. Although we may follow the rules based on consequences, we can, through practice, develop the habit of punctuality and a sense of responsibility and commitment.

In nurturing self-disciplined children, we need to establish boundaries and solid structures from which they might produce virtuous behaviors. Emile Durkheim, the esteemed nineteenth century sociologist, reminds us that *"...solely by imposing limits can a child be liberated."* Similarly, by imposing limits in schools through the creation of rules and procedures, students will cultivate the habits needed as prerequisites for becoming good citizens and practicing good habits of virtue.

Aristotle suggests this in the *Nicomachean Ethics* in which he describes two kinds of virtue. He delineates intellectual virtue as the contemplative side of virtue that is experienced through thinking and reflecting over ideas. Learning to think clearly and applying logic to ethical issues help enhance intellectual virtue.

Aristotle's second type of virtue, and the type this short work will consider, is moral virtue. This is sustained through the formulation and practice of good habits. This would include, but is not limited to, being punctual, respectful, courageous, responsible, and caring. By instilling these moral virtues or good habits in students, we are instituting rules that should be considered expectations of appropriate behavior leading to good citizenship. The procedures are the practices needed to spawn the habits of good citizenship.

If we think of this in terms of hierarchy, we would place the *virtues* such as respect, responsibility, and honesty on the top tier. The second tier would contain the *rules* we should follow to engender these virtues, while the third tier would hold the *procedures* or practices we must perform to create the habits which lead to a virtuous character.

> VIRTUES—The character traits we should strive to develop in students.
> RULES—The expectations designed for appropriate student behavior.
> PROCEDURES—The practices needed to develop the habits of following rules and developing good character.

Consider the following example:
> **Virtue** = Respect
> **Rule** = Treat all people with respect.

Procedures = Do not interrupt others when they are speaking. Practice active listening. Use polite language, such as *please* and *thank you,* to everyone.

Another way of looking at this process is provided by Dr. David Wangaard from the School for Ethical Education in Bridgeport, Connecticut. Dr. Wangaard uses expectations instead of listing the traits. He also generates procedures which lead to a formation of rules.

Consider the following example:

Expectations:

Students will model respectful behavior.

Procedures:

Students will be polite to others, e.g., saying please, thank you, yes, no. Students will practice active listening.

Rules:

Treat all people with respect.

Both processes, unfold when the proper environment is created. Educators are faced with the challenge of providing a nurturing climate in schools that accents the development of character in their students. The next section addresses how a school's climate is the pivotal matrix for germinating character development in its students.

THE IMPORTANCE OF CLIMATE IN CHARACTER BUILDING

Character develops within a social web or environment. The nature of that environment, the messages it sends to individuals, and the behaviors it encourages and discourages, are important factors to consider in character education. Clear rules of conduct, student ownership of those rules, a supportive environment and satisfaction resulting from complying with the norms of the environment shape behavior (p. 69).

Dr. James Leming

We can tell a great deal about a school's climate by talking to key people connected to the school. A central office supervisor is a great contact person who can provide the names of some excellent teachers who travel between schools teaching English as a second language, foreign language, art, music or other subjects. We could ask them to describe each school regarding:

1. Attentiveness of students;
2. Observed parental involvement; and
3. Working relationships with other staff.

Talking with the school secretary/registrar provides data about student attendance, discipline referrals and teacher absences. The number of absences and referrals indicates the degree of supportiveness existing in the school's environment. When the climate is nurturing, educators perform better and students learn more. Teacher absences might be affected by special circumstances, such as a serious illness or pregnancy, but in general, absences on Monday and Friday are significant indicators of low morale or burnout.

Talking with elective teachers, such as physical education, music, art, or vocational education, can reveal the nature of students' manners when they come to class. These teachers can answer questions like: Are the students orderly? Respectful? Caring towards others? Do they follow schools rules and procedures? Or do they come down the halls in a disorderly manner with little concern for others?

The climate of a school is a great reflection of its inhabitants. Generally, a school with an inviting climate has educators and students who enjoy being at school. Schools with good climates have people who want to build relationships with each other. Dr. Jim Sweeney, a nationally recognized expert in fostering a positive school climate, notes:

> Climate is a term used to describe how people feel about their school. It is a combination of beliefs, values, and attitudes shared by students, teachers, administrators, parents, bus drivers, office personnel, custodians, cafeteria workers, and others who play an important role in the life of the school. When a school has a "winning climate," people feel proud, connected, and committed. They support, help and care for each other. When the climate is right, there is a certain joy in coming to school, either to teach or to learn (p.1).

Suppose you work in a school similar to the school Dr. Sweeney describes. How would you describe the learning activities of the students in this winning climate? We might hypothesize that the students are involved in their learning; that they are enthusiastic knowledge-seekers and they exercise their natural curiosities to explore and reflect on their environment. In this climate, students strive to go above and beyond minimal academic standards and to develop character traits, such as respect and responsibility, which they will use throughout their lives.

Educators aid in this process through modeling appropriate social behavior with the understanding that not all good character is taught, some is caught through observation of others. Educators germinate seeds in students which will bear the fruit of good behavior. For some students, modeling good behavior and the statement of the rules are enough. Other students need to face consequences for their actions (more about this in Chapter 4) before they learn good behavior. A good school helps young people grow into good citizens through instruction, modeling, and an insistence on following rules for the betterment of everyone in the school.

When a school has a good climate, people interact and a community develops. This is what all educators and students deserve. In achieving this climate, a school must have rules and procedures that are followed and supported by both teachers and students. A good climate sets the stage for Aristotle's moral virtue to blossom. Consider the following scenarios regarding rules and procedures and their impact on school climate.

Scenario 1

A high school principal was very concerned about increasing noise and disturbances in the halls during class changes. Several students had been pushed down accidentally and stepped on. One suffered a broken arm. The school had rules and procedures that governed how students were to behave, but it seemed the students were not following the rules. The principal called on one of her peers to help analyze this problem. The peer and principal stood in the halls during a class change, which were extremely loud and disruptive. The peer asked to see the rules and procedures of the school, including those governing how students were to act during class changes. There were also rules and procedures governing the teacher's actions.

On further observation, the principal and peer noticed that the teachers were not standing in the hall during the class changes. They were not following the procedure of being in the hall to promote civil dialogue and to model caring towards the students. The hall contained ten teacher classrooms, but not one teacher was standing in the hall during the class changes.

At the next staff meeting, everyone expressed concern about the noise and potential for disturbances in the hall. The principal reviewed the rules and procedures of the school and asked how many teachers had been standing in the hall. Few hands were raised. She reminded them that the reason for being in the hall was to promote dialogue and model caring for the students. It was hoped that the students would then express civil dialogue and caring towards their peers and the teachers. Afterward, the teachers agreed to return to the hall during class changes.

In the meantime, the student government addressed this issue with their homeroom representatives. It was decided that the students should review their rules and procedures for proper behavior in the hall. Within a short period of time the students were quieter during the class changes. The students and teachers were exchanging greetings and small talk during the class changes. Together they were improving the climate of the school by following *their* rules and procedures. Through practice, habits of good behavior were being developed.

Scenario 2

An elementary school was having problems with its after-school bus students. A guidance counselor noticed that, on some days, the students came into the cafeteria and began work. On other days, the students came into the cafeteria and were loud and disruptive while they were waiting for the second bus.

After a week of observation, the counselor noted that the person on bus duty determined how the students acted. The counselor knew this should not occur because there were rules and procedures that stated how students were to act upon arriving in the cafeteria. The counselor continued to keep records and shared her observations with the principal and the Building Leadership Team (BLT). The BLT decided to place this concern on the faculty meeting agenda. The principal reviewed the rules and procedures teachers and students should follow upon entering the cafeteria.

The teachers and teacher assistants agreed that they must be consistent with their expectation and enforcement of the procedures. The teachers reviewed the procedures again with the students. To develop responsibility in completing all homework, each student was to come into the cafeteria and work without talking on homework for 20 minutes. After 20 minutes the staff would give permission to talk quietly. In a short period of time, all the students were working on their homework while they waited for the bus. When the staff were consistent in their expectations, the students responded. A better climate was created in the school through consistency with the rules and following the procedures.

Note what the two examples have in common: Both these examples have rules and procedures that govern how the students and teachers are supposed to act. The educators and students knew the rules and procedures, yet they had become slack in their practice, creating climate problems in their schools. They had failed to act with the total community in mind.

Perhaps the previous examples seem too simple. After all, excessive noise in the hall or in the after school-care waiting area may not be a major issue to some people. But the contradictory message to students is important: the standards were being ignored. Expecting students to be civil in the entire school environment is a reasonable expectation. Excessive noise may seem like a small problem, but it contributes to poor habits in the lives of students and subsequently the teachers.

Rules (the standards) and procedures (actions practiced and habits instilled to reach the standards) are essential for the smooth functioning of a school, but they will only be effective if they are consistently taught and practiced. We all value consistency; otherwise life is chaotic and unproductive.

Thirteen-year-old Jimmy, writing a letter to his father on Father's Day in Ann Landers, June 15, 1997 column, expresses gratitude for his parents' consistent rules:

> I like the way you don't let me get away with much. Sometimes I act mad when I don't get my way, but deep down I am glad you are strict. I would be scared to death if you let me do anything I want. I like that you and Mom agree on the rules around here. At Tommy's house, if his mom says he can't do something, he goes and asks his dad because he knows his dad will say OK just to get rid of him.

To develop the habits of good behavior that Jimmy writes about, we must be consistent with what we model and in what we expect. In Ken Beck and Jim Clark's *The Andy Griffith Show Book* (1985), Opie Taylor, Sheriff Andy Taylor's son in the popular 1960s television series, is a benefactor of consistent rules and modeling. Beck and Clark write:

> The younger Taylor knows exactly what his father expects of him, whether it be chores around the house or at the courthouse, or his conduct in the classroom or on the playground. Andy has taught Opie the importance of responsibility, respect and honesty.

In yet another example, a school faculty decides that it will allow teachers to determine whether or not students are tardy to class. One week later, disorder is rampant in the halls. Some teachers require the students to be in the class when the tardy bell rings. Others let students in the room and don't count them tardy five minutes after the tardy bell rings. What are the students learning? They learn that being punctual depends on who is judging. Punctuality is relative. Punctuality can be five minutes late or in the door as the bell rings. Is this what we want students to learn? Is this a habit we want them to develop? Is this a way to teach or model a virtue? Is this a way to build consensus? Is this the way to run a school?

If students are to develop the skills needed to be good citizens, then setting limits, being consistent, modeling what is expected, and determining practices that will enhance learning are essential. The next section focuses on the logistics needed to help foster good habits in students which can be accomplished through the establishment, practice and following of rules and procedures.

REVIEW

1   Life is regulated by rules and procedures.

2   According to Aristotle, there are two types of virtue: intellectual, which develops the contemplative side of virtue; and moral virtue, which is sustained and developed by the formulation and practice of good habits and/or virtues.

3   We must determine the virtues or good habits we wish to develop and formulate the habits or practices which, if students and adults practice, will contribute to the development of that virtue.

4   A positive school climate which emphasizes "knowing, loving, and doing the good" is essential.

RULES & PROCEDURES

2

CLEAR RULES OF CONDUCT SHAPE POSITIVE STUDENT BEHAVIOR

Years ago, I attended a conference between a parent of a primary grade student and several educators. The child was highly undisciplined and causing much concern within the classroom. After discussions, I asked the mother to explain her discipline policy. She stated that she did not discipline her child very much at home, for fear it would stifle his creativity. I then asked her to tell me the name of a highly creative person who was not disciplined.

We acknowledged that discipline can enhance creativity through establishing comfortable parameters for a child to function in, and we discussed how parameters aid in restoring order and providing a harmonious environment.

Over time, the child's behavior gradually improved in school. The mother informed the conference participants that she was doing a better job at home in stating rules and helping the child institute good procedures regarding appropriate behavior. She was consistent in holding her son accountable for the consequences of failing to follow directions or meet expectations. The school environment augmented this work by further reinforcing his emerging self-control.

Being disciplined and able to follow rules, learned through the practice of procedures, is desirable for all children. We cannot empower children to think and act properly unless the children are disciplined (understand the rules) and have developed good habits (learn and practice good procedures). Fortunately, we are programmed at birth to grow and develop good habits of caring and concern. William Damon, in his work, *Greater Expectations* (1995), notes:

> The seeds of the moral sense are sown at conception, and its roots are firmly established at birth. Every infant enters this world prepared to respond socially, and in a moral manner, to others. Every child has the capacity to acquire moral character. The necessary emotional response systems, budding cognitive awareness, and personal dispositions are there from the start. Although, unfortunately, not every child grows into a responsible and caring person, the potential to do so is native to every member of the species (p. 132).

What Damon so eloquently points out is that the wiring is there for the development of good moral citizens. He argues that there are four overlapping processes present and active at birth: moral emotions, such as empathy, fear and guilt; moral judgment to determine conduct in matters of justice, care, truthfulness, responsibility and ethical duty; social cognition to relate to the social world; and self–understanding to glean awareness of our past, present and future self and to master self–control.

Yet, having the wiring alone doesn't guarantee that a child will develop into a good citizen. We may approach this by stating that the capacity to acquire moral character is necessary, but it is not sufficient to the development of a good character—a good person.

To round out the development of a good, civil person, we must add instruction, modeling and practice. This requires caring adults and a consistent environment that seeks to develop respectful, responsible children/students. Through education and modeling, we socialize children to become adults. The truth can cause a parent or teacher much chagrin at times. Children learn what they see and hear!

Several years ago my daughter, then three years old, and I were riding in a car near our home. A car pulled out in front of us which I narrowly missed. Without thinking, I blurted out a choice line of words. Several weeks later we had another near accident. I didn't need to say the words; my daughter did! She modeled what she had heard and seen.

However, not everyone believes that we should "socialize" children and model appropriate behavior. The philosopher Rousseau maintained that children should be children before they become adults. He recognized that children have their own unique ways of thinking and feeling. Common sense tells us this. However, his laissez-faire approach to child rearing, described in great detail in his work, *Emile,* states that children should not be contaminated by the world. He maintained that, left to their own accords, they will develop into morally sensitive individuals through their intuitions, experiences and feelings. Of course there is no evidence to support this. Rousseau may have correctly gleaned that children have the seeds of morality, but he failed to recognize the importance that interactions with caring adults play in the development of the good child.

Daniel Goleman, in his book, *Emotional Intelligence (1995),* recorded that two-year-old children who have been raised in nurturing homes will try to comfort a friend who is crying. Children who have been abused or neglected early in their life tend to yell at or hit crying children. Without a range of positive experiences from nurturing parents, these neglected children had no compassionate or comforting skills to call upon.

Even with the types of incidents Goleman describes above, coupled with the apparent flaws in the laissez-faire child-rearing theory (the policy of letting people act without direction or interference), proponents of Rousseau have gained steam by stretching the work of Jean Piaget's educational development concept into the so-called "child-centered" classroom.

William Damon recognized this distortion of Piaget's work when he states that, in educational terminology, child centered "...generally means a laissez-faire approach that allows children to proceed at their own pace, pursue their own interests, and learn from their own actions. It follows from what is known as a 'constructivist' perspective on learning—a position also widely attributed to Piaget (p. 102)."

Piaget believed that children construct their own learning and meaning of the world, but that does not mean we should allow children, especially in primary grades, to determine what and how they should learn.

Damon adds, "In truth, Piaget was not only a constructivist but also an *interactionist.* When Piaget wrote that children learn through their own actions, he did not mean that they learn in a vacuum. Essential to the learning process, as Piaget formulated it, was *feedback* from the child's actions to the real world (p. 103)...Simply put, children cannot learn wholly on their own; for intellectual growth, they need to be instructed, prodded, challenged, corrected, and assisted by people who are trying to teach them something (p. 105)." Children need love. They also need adults who act as a moral compass.

Child-centered does not mean child-controlled, and while the needs of the child are paramount, we should apply what we know about how children learn to the classroom. We must instruct and lead. This applies to the intellect as well as the moral or social processes. We must dialogue, and insist on practices that lead to the formation of a good learning and caring community.

In a society that follows certain conventions and requires children to interact with adults, allowing a child to pursue his/her own interests when s/he desires will not work. Children need time to explore ideas and play, but they also need to develop the habits of being respectful, responsible and caring from our modeling and teaching these standards.

Students need guidance and standards by which to assess their responses. Simply stating what we feel is, by itself, not necessarily enough to sprout good values. Feeling good about a response does not make the response acceptable. Sometimes a statement or a cherished belief is wrong or, at least, misleading.

In cherishing children, we realize that our obligation to them includes helping them acquire good character. In so doing, we are helping them learn self-control and respect for self and others. We must connect the cables in their "wiring." Damon adds:

> Children must learn to cope with stubborn realities that will not change, as the children's moods and feelings change, and that will not vanish when the children's complaints grow loud enough. Failing to give children firm rules and guidelines is a sure way to breed arrogance and disrespect. It leads to another facet of the inflated sense of self-importance that is fed by our culture's over emphasis on self-esteem (p. 79.)

A good way to insure that students become disciplined is to construct rules and procedures, which if followed, are beneficial to the smooth functioning of a school and the character development of the students. To learn more about this we turn to Dr. Harry and Tripi Wong's work, *The First Days of School* (1991). The Wongs' note:

1. The most successful classes are those where the teacher has a clear idea of what is expected from the students and the students know what the teacher expects from them.

2. Expectations can be stated as rules.

3. Rules are expectations of appropriate student behavior.

4. After thorough deliberation, decide on your rules and write them down or post them before the first days of school.

5. Communicate clearly to your students what you expect as appropriate behavior.

6. It is easier to maintain good behavior than to change inappropriate behavior that has become established.

7. Rules immediately create a work-oriented atmosphere.

8. Rules create a strong expectation about the things that are important to you (p. 143).

In other words, rules let students know what is valued in a classroom. The Wongs indicate that there are different kinds of rules. **Specific rules** are exacting in nature. They tell you what to do, and you do not need any additional explanation. For example, "Pick up the trash around your desk at the end of the class period" does not need any additional explanation. Another specific rule might be "Keep your hands, feet and objects to yourself." These rules stand by themselves.

The same applies to rules like "Place your homework in the basket when you walk into the class." Provide a basket. Label it *Homework* and put it in a convenient location where students entering the classroom can't miss seeing it. Have them put their homework in the basket. After several practices, the students are accustomed to the procedure.

General rules are different. They prescribe what we *ought* to do, but they don't give specific details about how to follow the rules. For example, the general rule "Treat all persons with respect" provides a fine prescription as to how a child should act, but it does not tell the child what s/he should do to exhibit mastery of the virtue or the expectation.

Young children and adolescents can be confused about what it means to treat someone with respect. They may not know *how* to do this. Have you ever talked with a child who honestly didn't know what he had done wrong, or how his actions were inappropriate? In Chapter 3, we will learn more about practicing procedures that will help the child develop the habits which lead to civility and avoiding confusion.

REVIEW

1 We are wired with the potential to be a good person. To complete the "circuit," children need moral modeling and instruction.

2 Children left on their own will not learn to be a moral person. They need feedback and interaction with caring adults.

3 A child–centered classroom does not mean child–controlled. As adults, we are in charge of insuring that a good caring and learning community exists.

4 Rules facilitate the development of a good climate, for children and adults, by helping all know what is valued.

3

RULES & PROCEDURES

PROCEDURES BREATHE LIFE INTO RULES

P rocedures are different than rules. While specific rules tell us what to do, and general rules prescribe what we *ought to do*, procedures describe how *things are done*. They are the practices or steps needed to follow the rules. Ask yourself the following question: When do students generally get in trouble—during times of direct instruction or during transitions?

Like most educators, you will probably answer during *transitions*. Such a problem is a procedural one, demanding clear-cut practices to resolve it. Assume that a classroom/school has several specific rules and one general rule: "Treat everyone with respect." Many students may be unsure what this means. They may need to practice showing respect to own the habit of respecting others. The following rule is presented as an expectation of appropriate student behavior.

RULE: TREAT EVERYONE WITH RESPECT

What are the procedures students need to practice to acquire the habit of treating people with respect? If we start with being respectful of others in the halls, we establish that students and teachers will exhibit quietness in the halls and do not interrupt the learning opportunities of others.

To develop the habit of treating others with respect while walking in the halls, we need to do the following:

PROCEDURES

1   Walk on the right side of the hall.

2   Walk quietly in the halls. In middle and high school, talk, not yell in the hall when changing classes. [Because elementary students move throughout the school all day long, they should move quietly in the halls so others are not disturbed. One primary school has students practice talking quietly in the hall when an adult is talking to them.]

3   Hold the door for those walking behind you to prevent the door from slamming.

4   Avoid aggressive behavior by keeping your hands to yourself.

NOW YOU TRY

The general rule is: **Respect Others.** Incorporate procedures that will help students practice respect in the classroom. What procedures do you want your students to practice? (You may have a specific rule, "Keep hands, feet and objects to yourself" as a procedure. This is fine for it tells a student specifically what to do and by its practice leads to the habit of being respectful.)

1.

2.

3.

4.

5.

What is another general rule or expectation of appropriate behavior you want students to follow in your classroom? What procedures do they need to learn to develop the habit of following the rule?

GENERAL RULE:

Procedures:

1.

2.

3.

4.

5.

Notice how practicing these procedures can help students learn to be respectful to others. Through practice, respect becomes an acquired habit. The same approach applies to any other positive attribute we wish students and educators to adopt. Practice of the virtue makes perfect!!

Look at the rule and procedures you listed above. If students followed these procedures, would they practice actions and develop habits that would allow them to follow the rule? Some educators may argue that following rules and procedures might not be all that important. After all, in the total scheme of things, what does the development of small positive habits do for students? What is the big deal about holding the door open for someone or being respectful toward others in a classroom? James Q. Wilson, in his work, *The Moral Sense* (1993) states:

> ...habits, routine ways of acting, each rather unimportant
> in itself, but taken together, producing action on behalf
> of quite important sensibilities. For example: the habit of

courtesy (which over the long run alerts us to the feelings of others), the habit of punctuality (which disposes us to be dutiful in the exercise of our responsibilities and confirms to others that we have a sense of duty), and the habit of practice (by which we master skills and proclaim to others that we are capable of excellence) (p. 241).

The little habits, practiced daily, help a school function smoothly and mold the character of youth and adults, which makes a great deal of difference in the life of the child. Rules and procedures "set the table" for all future character developing efforts. Remember our task is to help facilitate the development of good student habits through the use of rules and procedures.

An excellent methodology to help teachers organize the practice of procedures is provided in the book *Organizing and Managing the Elementary School Classroom (1981),* published by the Research and Development Center for Teacher Education at the University of Texas at Austin. This work recognizes that procedures or actions designed to develop habits in students are important to help them learn to follow rules. Observe how this project uses rules and procedures to help educators focus on what they must consider to facilitate the development of good student habits:

1. **Be polite and helpful.** This may be worded in various ways (e.g., be considerate of others; be courteous). Children must be given examples for this rule to have meaning. They must learn how to be polite and helpful in dealing with adults and each other.

2. **Take care of your school.** This is another very general rule that the teacher must think through before using. The teacher may want to include positive examples, such as picking up trash in the halls or on the school grounds, returning library books on time, and/or such rigidly stated things as not marking on walls, desks, or school books. The teacher must be sure to discuss and follow up with the class whatever detailed behavior is expected from this rule as well as consequences for not following the rule.

Both the Wongs' and the Texas Project reveal that just stating the rules isn't enough to develop good character in students. Teachers must determine the procedures needed for students to understand, practice, and develop good habits that make following rules a natural part of their day. State the rules and then make some general comments about the rules. Afterward, the faculty could determine the procedures needed to develop the habits of following the rules. The Texas project could very well be a model for school-wide rules and procedures.

So far, the discussion has been about rules and procedures being in the domain of educators. Can students help in determining rules and procedures? Absolutely! Students know about the importance of rules as early as preschool. They also may know what they ought to do. The following approaches utilize students' input:

Scenario One:

Cynthia Vincent, an elementary teacher in Hickory, North Carolina, implemented procedures based on her rules regarding students being respectful, responsible, and caring toward themselves and others. She started out the school year by writing the words Respect, Responsibility and Caring on her blackboard. She then asked each student what they did at home and at school to practice being respectful, responsible, and caring. Each idea was discussed in depth and afterward, the students created art that illustrated them practicing Respect, Responsibility, and Caring. Ms. Vincent modified her and her students' ideas into a list of procedures they all would follow in the classroom and hall.

On the second day of school, these students began practicing their procedures, diligently continuing through the week. After the first week, the students had developed many of the habits that would allow them to be successful in school. An environment that was good for students as well as the teacher evolved.

Ms. Vincent continued the focus by having a meeting at the beginning of each school day in order for students to talk about what they could do to be respectful and responsible that day. Time was taken to thank others for what they had done the previous day.

Any "backsliding" was discussed over a class meeting.

The students were asked to reflect on what had been occurring in the classroom, and the rules and procedures were reviewed for further reinforcement. Procedures that were not being followed consistently were highlighted and extra effort was required.

By implementing procedures for proper behavior in class, Ms. Vincent had a wonderful environment from which to teach and the students had greater opportunities to learn. Finally, as students continued their excellent behavior, they were recognized for their success. Celebrating excellence is important and breeds more successes.

Scenario Two:

Booker T. Washington High School in Pensacola, Florida used high school students' input to determine some procedures based on the five school rules they created to foster a better climate for learning. Shirley Bordelon, a guidance counselor at the school, provides the following description of their efforts.

Teachers, administrators, staff, and 23 Student Government Association leaders and Core Values Team members were randomly divided into groups of 14 to 16 people, with at least one or two students in every group. A trained facilitator, Pam Shelton, directed the entire process.

First, the groups brainstormed to identify problems and concerns. Each group developed five general rules and wrote them on a flip chart. When each group had completed this, similar rules were combined, and one list of five rules was drafted. The five rules adopted were:

- Show respect for yourself, others and property.
- Demonstrate personal responsibility.
- Obey laws concerning drugs and alcohol.
- Be honest in all you do.
- Contribute to a positive school environment.

The students selected the rule on drugs and alcohol. Just two weeks before, an outstanding sophomore had been killed in an alcohol/high speed related car accident. Another Booker T. Washington student was the driver. Some teachers (new to the faculty) did not feel this rule was appropriate. Much discussion and disagreement took place.

The facilitator later stated that this was the one point she could feel control of the group waning. In the midst of teachers confronting one another on whether this was an appropriate rule, two students stood side-by-side, held hands and cried as they addressed the group. In essence, this is what they said, "We just lost a friend in an alcohol-related accident. We KNOW what teens do on weekends now, and we know alcohol is a BIG problem. All we ask is that you work with us. We know we can't stop all this behavior, but if you will join us, perhaps, together we can make an impact on some. We don't want to lose another classmate."

Many were crying by this time. They sat down, and teachers and staff began clapping—louder and louder. Needless to say, one of the five rules adopted was related to alcohol.

The custodian was involved in the development of the rules. It was especially touching when one of the students "high fived" the custodian. It was gratifying to all of the teachers to have been a part of the process and witness all of the mutual respect being displayed.

The group knew this was only the beginning. One morning the students were given the task of developing three procedures under each of the five general rules. Directions were given over the television broadcasting system by the SGA president. Each first-period classroom held a class meeting to establish three specific procedures that described what the students should do to follow the general rules. The teachers facilitated the process, which took about an hour.

Each class then selected two "core values representatives" to bring the procedures to the cafeteria. The next day, during an early-release day from school, approximately 160 students were grouped randomly at tables in a huge semi-circle. Two very outgoing teachers facilitated the process, with the assistance of six students who are Escambia County Core Value Team members—a group of students who travel throughout the schools and community talking about the importance of having good core values. Basically, they followed the same process that the faculty and students had done earlier when developing the five general rules.

The student body was representative of Advanced Placement to special education, as well as equal representation of gender, race, and socioeconomic levels. What these students did was incredible! They shared ideas, defended their choices, questioned others and learned how to come to consensus. They became so enthusiastically involved that the processes were not complete when school was dismissed at 10:30 a.m. on the early-release day. The principal allowed the same group of students to meet again on Friday morning for the first time block (90 minutes) to complete their work.

Shirley Bordelon notes: "Students claim ownership in rules and practices when they are the authors. With a little guidance, I believe they did a much better job than a group of us adults could have done. Their rules are from the heart—that was obvious during the process.

"It just reinforced what I already believe. Our youth are the greatest. Give them Respect, give them a chance to assume Responsibility, treat them with Equality, react to them with Honesty and Integrity, and they will respond with tremendous Patriotism. B.T. Washington High School is a school reaching for realms beyond what could have been imagined three years ago. We are *indeed a school on the move in the right direction with our students.*"

This school's approach to character development could serve as a guide for other middle and high school staff wanting to create the same processes. It appears that the students knew that, in developing these rules, they would not be limiting their control; rather, they would be assisting in creating the type of school environment they desired.

The process would be the same with elementary students as described in Approach One. Teachers, administrators and parents usually start the process, followed by the input of the students to establish the practices. This is the beginning of children creating their own destinies.

REVIEW

1 Rules are expectations of appropriate student behavior. Procedures are the practices needed to develop the habits of good behavior or virtues.

2 Children need to be disciplined. By this we mean students need to follow rules through utilizing agreed upon procedures. Discipline helps them develop good habits. This is made easier since children have the "wiring" for such behavior at birth.

3 There are both specific and general rules. Specific rules tell us exactly what we should do (e.g., "Put your homework in the basket as you walk in the classroom door.") General rules prescribe how we ought to act (e.g., "Respect Others").

4 To avoid confusion with rules, and especially general rules, we must include procedures that help to develop the habits needed to follow the rules.

5 Students can help in this endeavor, but they are not participants in a total democracy. The educational establishment is ultimately responsible for insuring an environment where learning can occur; however, this does not minimize student contributions, nor their abilities to focus on key rules and procedures.

6 It is helpful to post the procedures stating how students are expected to behave. Far too often we post rules without the procedures. Both are needed to remind students of good behavior.

RULES & PROCEDURES

4

THE USE OF
CONSEQUENCES
IN BUILDING CHARACTER

My involvement with school districts around the country reveals that the majority of school personnel want to help children develop good habits. They want to address rules and procedures that offer good practices and hold students accountable. This chapter will clarify the importance of rules and procedures; offering guidelines on how to use the consequences of not following rules and procedures to encourage good habits in their students.

This chapter will not satisfy everyone. Some may argue that if we let kids find their own way with minimal adult supervision, they will grow into solid students and citizens. There are times when a child may need less adult supervision. Adults must provide more autonomy for the child as he matures. However, this does not divorce adults from the life of the child. James Q. Wilson in *The Moral Sense* (1993) notes:

> Testing limits is a way of asserting selfhood. Maintaining limits is a way of asserting community. If the limits are asserted weakly, uncertainly, or apologetically, their effects must surely be weaker than if they are asserted boldly, confidently and persuasively (p. 9).

The expectations of appropriate behavior should be expected and exemplified by the child even when s/he is away from immediate supervision.

An acquaintance told me that, when her teenagers leave the house, she inquires where her teens are going, who they will be with, and when they will be home. The teens also leave with one rule: "Have responsible fun—no drinking, drugs, or sex!" The teens laugh about this, but their parents' insistence that habits of respect and responsibility to others and themselves is reinforced by this reminder. Children need the constant involvement of parents and other adults to act as moral compasses.

There are various strategies we can use to represent this compass. We can talk with our children or students. Sharing ideas and stories is important in the lives of children. We can insist on the development of good habits in our children at home, in the community and school, and have consequences for behaviors we deem inappropriate. Some may feel that consequences or punishment of children are unnecessary, that we should just dialogue with them and model what we feel is important.

Modeling and practicing are important. Other times, instilling traits like good manners and courtesy call for continual practice. The role of dialoguing in enacting rules and procedures is important, yet, there are also times when the consequences of one's actions must be confronted. Learning there are consequences for certain behaviors, and that these consequences may be called punishment, has a place in building character in our youth.

Briefly, we can examine the definitions of punishment and consequences and see that they are related terms. Synonyms of punishment are discipline and correction. According to *The New World Dictionary of the American Language: Second College Edition*, (1986):

> ...*discipline* suggests punishment that is intended to control or to establish habits of self-control [to discipline a naughty child]; *correct* suggests punishment for the purpose of overcoming faults [to correct unruly pupils].

This is exactly what punishment should mean for schools: to help students establish self-control which enables them to overcome faults that may result in a disruption of the learning environment for themselves and others.

Consequence is defined as "a result of an action, process, etc., outcome, effect. 2. a logical result or conclusion: inference." Synonyms of consequence are "effect or value." For example, if one assumes the consequences of one's transactions, one will "accept the results of one's actions." Awareness of consequences implies that, if one chooses to misbehave, one will accept the logical result (punishment) for one's actions. In this case, consequences are the punishment, and punishment reflects the consequences.

We could argue that students who continue to skip classes in middle or high school will not be allowed to easily make up their work is an illogical consequence. "If they can't quickly make up their work they will fail the course," voices a concerned parent. The teacher argues, "Skipping school results in students being behind in their work. We should provide ample opportunity for them to make up their work." I see the point but I must answer, "Rubbish!" They have *chosen* to skip school. Allowing them to *easily* make-up their work may reinforce the behavior. It is the student's job to get the assignments and make-up the work. It is not the teacher's job to bend over backwards to help. If the behavior continues, then additional privileges of the student should be revoked.

My argument is that attending school is a privilege. The privilege assumes that one does one's duty by attending school. If making up school work is made easy for the students who choose to skip school, then what is the consequence for skipping school? It appears the burden is placed on the teacher, not the student. What is the child learning? Will this learned behavior carry into the world of work? Clearly, there are exceptions but exceptions must not become the rule. The development of habits of attendance and the responsibility of doing good work in schools are lifelong skills. The school's role is to reinforce punctuality and accountability. Rules should be honored or consequences otherwise faced.

In another example, a student curses at a teacher. (The age at which the cursing occurs is important. Young children might not know it is wrong, but they can be taught of its unacceptability). This is a serious offense in which the student needs to face the consequences. We can talk to the student and discover what caused him to present such an outburst. We can suggest ways to avoid this behavior in the future. But there must be some consequences for the action, or we are telling him, along with twenty-five other students, that cursing at a teacher is acceptable behavior, which it is not. There is a time for counseling/talking, and there is a time for consequences/punishment.

Some maintain that a child who continually challenges the rules of a school is begging for help. If this is so, the school should do all it can to help by providing counseling and support. In providing the support to the student, the school must also insist on adherence to following the rules or facing the consequences. Expectations of appropriate behavior during the class period should not be compromised by tolerating disruptive behavior from a student with underlying personal problems.

Educators frequently ask me if I *really* believe in enforcing consequences that result in punishment. My answer is affirmative if a student chooses to break the rules or refuses to follow the procedures established in school. The key word here is *chooses*. An atypical situation might be a severely handicapped child whose abilities to make decisions may be compromised, contributing to various outbursts.

As educators, we are obligated to meet the educational needs of all students. They expect the administration and faculty to be consistent, caring, and fair in providing a favorable learning environment. What's important is insuring a safe, consistent environment for children to learn both the academics and social skills needed for good citizenship.

The majority of students know what they are doing and choose to do it, even those students we consider to be "emotionally handicapped." My experiences with K-12 have exposed me to educators who have created caring learning environments with almost any kind of child in their class— no matter what the child's classification.

Children naturally respond well in classes where teachers have high expectations, caring environments and solid instructional strategies that include the practice of rules and procedures designed to help students achieve academic and social goals. These teachers let all students know they are responsible for their work and their behavior, recognizing that most students, even those with behavioral problems, want to do well and be liked by others.

Anne Jenkins is a prime example of a teacher with high expectations. She stresses parental involvement and discipline with her twenty kindergarten students at Diggs Elementary School in Winston-Salem, North Carolina. According to Kristin Scheve, writing for the *Winston-Salem Journal* (June 7, 1997), parents praised Jenkins for her emphasis on discipline and expressed pride that their children were already reading at the end of the school year.

Skilled educators like Jenkins encourage the practice of regular procedures, knowing firsthand that the procedures may not go smoothly with all students. These teachers are also willing to use consequences for students who choose to disrupt the learning environment for others. Students with behavioral problems are expected to achieve steady improvement through the school year. In this safe environment, most students will make progress, even if their home lives are deteriorating. The classroom becomes the basis of this stability. Using punishment/consequence is the last alternative, but it is an alternative that can and should be used.

Whether it is one teacher at a time or middle school teams who are committed to providing a structured caring environment for their students, both have consistent school-wide procedures they follow to engender warm, learning environments.

Middle school teams at Arndt Middle School in Hickory, North Carolina are responsible for office referrals dropping from nearly ten per day to less than one per day over a five-year period. The teams work hard to develop a consistent school-wide structure which insures a caring environment for the students. Students who choose to misbehave in classes "face the team." Misbehaving students must sit down with the team members during team planning. The principal or guidance counselor may attend the conference, along with the elective teacher who is also committed to the process.

The "face the team" meeting consists of serious discussions with the student. It is not intended to be a pleasant conference. Its clinical function is to determine what action must be taken to stop the present behavior. The teachers talk with the student, but are very firm and polite about their expectations. They remind the student of the consequences that will occur if disruptive behavior continues. The school's data indicate that most students (over 80 percent) who "face the team" never need to come back to a session.

Students who still choose not to follow procedures, even after efforts of educators, must face the consequences. Educators must not shy away from punishment when students show a disregard for civility, like striking another student.

Edward Wynne and Kevin Ryan, in their book *Reclaiming Our Schools: A Handbook on Teaching Character, Academics, and Discipline,* 2nd Edition (1997), recognize the important role of consequences for students who choose to misbehave. The authors emphasize that effective punishments or consequences must have certain characteristics:

1. They must be clearly disliked by students—they must deter.

2. They must not absorb large amounts of school resources (e.g., schools cannot afford to assign a full-time paid adult monitor for each disobedient pupil).

3. They must be capable of being applied in "doses" of increasing severity.

4. They must not be perceived as cruel.

5. In public schools, they often must be applicable without strong cooperation from the parent of the pupil involved.

6. They must be able to be applied quickly—the next day, or even within one minute of the infraction, instead of the next week (p. 98).

The authors provide a long list of effective punishments or consequences. Some of their ideas are:

1. Subjecting pupils to before-or after-school detention within 24 hours of their violation (or, as one school found, Saturday detentions for more serious offenses, since they interrupted student's Saturday games and jobs).

2. Providing an in-school suspension in a designated room, supervised by a stern monitor, with chitchat prohibited and students assigned to do their missed class work.

3. Sharply and suddenly (and sometimes publicly) criticizing individual pupils for particular immediate acts of misconduct, such as treating another student harshly.

4. Having erring pupils write notes to their parents explaining their misconduct, and having them promptly return the notes, signed by their parents.

5. Automatically calling the police whenever any student's conduct violates the criminal law (p. 100).

You may disagree with Wynne and Ryan's selection of consequences. But would it not be unconscionable to allow students to act inappropriately time after time, when practicing character traits such as punctuality, courtesy and responsibility will help them in their lives? If modeling, practicing, teacher dialoguing, and peer pressure don't work, then consequences must be utilized.

The authors offer many other outstanding examples of consequences for refusing to follow rules and procedures, but, caution us to be fair in meting out consequences. Being fair, in this instance, means following school or school board policies and treating all students the same.

This doesn't mean that we shouldn't consider the circumstances resulting in a child's misconduct. A student who is going through a rough time may need extra attention. Staff should be made aware of these situations. Peer helpers can be enlisted to spend additional time with the student. Our main thrust is assisting all students and providing them with nurturing environments from which to learn. Still, consequences for inappropriate behavior must be considered and applied.

If cursing at a teacher is an offense that results in a three-to five-day suspension, then suspend the student. You may counsel him/her before the suspension and continue this after the suspension, but the suspension must occur. This is fair and motivates the child to learn appropriate ways to channel his/her anger before serious problems arise.

If consistent rules and procedures aren't being followed, particularly at the high school and middle school levels, then students will spot inequities as if they were neon-blinking signs on a roadway. The following example addresses the issue of consistency:

> Football is very important for the students and the community at Main High School. A senior player on the football team, Will, broke a school rule involving skipping class, which earned him a one-day suspension. Unfortunately, he broke this rule on a Friday, and since he was suspended that day (actually any suspension during a week results in a suspension for the remainder of that week's after-school activities), he could not participate in the football game. This was especially difficult since it was homecoming night, but he knew what would happen if he broke the rule.
>
> Several weeks later during the league championship games, Tom, the quarterback, was caught skipping class. The principal decided to hold off the suspension until Monday and allow Tom to quarterback for the team on Friday. Since they did not play the following week, the team would not be hurt.

Word seeped out to the students, who became angry about the unfair application of the consequences. They wanted to win the football game, but fair was fair. If Will had been suspended for that offense, then Tom should also face immediate suspension. The students took their case to the community and eventually the school board. They spoke of fairness and modeling of consistency. In essence, the principal lost the respect of the students and much of the faculty. He resigned at the end of the year.

There may have been underlying reasons why both students cut class. They might not have liked the class; they might not have studied for a test. Such reasons, though, don't justify cutting class. If cutting class results in a one-day suspension, then enforce the consequence. The students at Main High School "learned" that who you are determines how you will be treated from the principal's handling of this incident. If we truly want a "level playing field" for all students, then we have to make every effort to be consistent.

This issue of consistency is not just an administrative problem. It extends to teachers throughout the school. Elementary teachers face special problems with students who are in the halls all day, going to dance, foreign language classes, P.E., music, art, special education, etc. These teachers' consistent practice of procedures enable students to move back and forth in an orderly way.

Young students who are unable to follow the procedures in the beginning may need additional opportunities to develop the habits that will enable them to be successful. However, if they continue to disrupt the classroom environment, appropriate punishment should occur. Many primary teachers have found that not allowing children time to play at recess, and using this time instead to develop better habits of behavior, is a powerful deterrent. This punishment is not cruel, but it does make a powerful point. The child knows if he chooses to misbehave, recess will not be an option.

Middle schools also have special areas of concern because of the team framework from which they work. Teams can consist of two to five teachers who must try to develop consistent rules and procedures that are used and followed by all team students and teachers. Clearly, they must all follow school rules, but they may have specific team procedures. This helps insure consistency throughout the school day.

From an administrative point of view, if one teacher in the middle school team has far more office referrals than other members of the team, then this teacher might need some assistance in becoming more consistent in following established rules, procedures, and consequences. If it were a constant student problem, then the number of office referrals would be the same for all team members.

We must also assess the climate of the class to determine if it is an inviting one for students and adults. Is there genuine love between the teacher and the students? Remember, though it is impossible to like every child we teach, we are required to *love* every child we teach. Notice the difference. If we simply like children, we can excuse poor behavior just as we excuse poor behavior of some friends. But if we love students, we must help them do the right thing by modeling, talking, sharing and, if necessary, punishing. Therefore, does this teacher care about the students? If not, then the teacher needs more assistance.

Adding to Wynne's and Ryan's assessments on effective consequences is the use of "time-out." Generally speaking, time-out involves the teacher or the student through his/her own initiative, removing herself from a trying situation to assess and determine the right course of action. During time-out, a child may quietly sit and reflect on the previous events. The child can contemplate and, if necessary, write what is needed to rejoin the group in a more controlled manner. Depending on the age and maturity of the child, the child may rejoin the group without permission of the teacher or may need to talk with the teacher and describe her plan of action before rejoining the group. The focus on time-out should be on the student determining, perhaps with the help of a teacher, the appropriate steps to take to insure success in the group once again.

Diane Chelsom Gossen in her book *Restitution: Restructuring School Discipline* (1992), recommends restitution, having a student "make right" a particular wrong, as another method of possible punishments. One of the best examples on restitution can be viewed in episode 101, titled *Opie the Birdman,* on the Andy Griffith Show videos. Richard Kelly writing in *The Andy Griffith Show* (1981) describes Opie's careless actions and punishment:

> ...Opie, after being warned by his father to be careful
> how he used his new slingshot, carelessly killed a mother
> bird, leaving her babies helpless. Andy goes to Opie's
> room, and outside the window can be heard the cries of
> the little birds. Andy says, "I'm not going to give you a

whipping." He turns and opens the window and says, "Do you hear that? That's them young birds chirping for their mama that's never coming back. And you just listen to that for awhile."

Opie had to learn how to rear the three young birds, which became his restitution for accidentally killing their mother. As a result, Opie inherited two important character by-products: respect for life and a responsibility for his actions.

In *Restitution: Restructuring School Discipline* (1992), Gossen argues that teachers should encourage children to seek solutions to problems that would normally demand teacher intervention or consequences. For example, a child wrongs another child. The teacher does not immediately punish the child. Instead, the child who committed the offense works to make things right with the offended child, just as Opie made things right with the baby birds. A child who is capable of restitution must have several characteristics:

1. S/he must have a sense of right and wrong.
2. S/he must acknowledge that s/he did wrong to another.
3. S/he must be capable of developing an action which will make the wrong right and this action must be agreed upon by the offended and the teacher.

There is always an exception, and here it involves students who are unable or unwilling to admit infractions. In these cases, teacher-enforced consequences are still necessary, especially since some actions need immediate intervention. Students who have never been taught what it means to be respectful of others or be responsible for their own actions are at a disadvantage. This is why educators must take the time to go over rules and procedures with students at the beginning of each year and solicit student input and agreement over the importance of the rules and procedures needed to insure a good climate.

Extensive practice may be necessary for younger students. Older students, who have been in a character-developing environment emphasizing the practice of good rules and procedures, should be encouraged to continue their habits. Newcomers should receive an orientation session on the school's rules and procedures facilitated by the principal, assistant principal, counselor, teacher, or peers. Perhaps the best method is to have a combination of the above educators working to make students and their parents aware of the rules, procedures and if necessary, the consequences within the school environment.

REVIEW

1   Punishment and consequences are not dirty words. There are times when students must be punished for their actions.

2   Punishment must not be cruel and demeaning. This does not mean that it should be ineffective. It just means that we should treat the person with respect. (If you wonder if you can always do this, take heart with the comment of a British member of Parliament who once told a fellow lawmaker that he would treat him like a gentleman not because his fellow lawmaker was a gentleman, but because *he* was one!)

3   The punishment must be administered promptly. It makes little sense to issue punishment for an incident that occurred days ago.

4   The climate of the classroom can aid or stunt the development of good procedures and habits.

5   Some students may have the ability to "restitute" others for their offenses. If you can agree upon the restitution, this is a good lesson for students to learn.

6   What we have learned about rules and procedures and motivational theory thus far will help us to develop our own practices to cultivate character awareness in students.

RULES & PROCEDURES

5

Initiating Rules and Procedures in Your School

What character traits or positive habits should students have when they leave your school? Your school may have already adopted a list of character traits for good citizenship from your district office. If not, you can initiate the process by sharing with peers and community members various character traits to consider.

The Character Counts Coalition is a national association that has the support of 80 leading character-building organizations such as the YMCA, 4-H, Boy and Girl Scouts of America, and the American Federation of Teachers. This coalition considers trustworthiness, respect, responsibility, caring, fairness and citizenship as Six Pillars of Character worthy of cultivating in our children. These pillars might meet your needs, as the traits are universally appealing and can guide your efforts in developing rules and procedures. You will be on solid ground by making the six pillars your foundation, even if the school or district adds additional traits.

As a staff member, you would select a character trait and ask a question such as "What practices are needed to help students learn to act responsibly towards themselves and others?" This list of traits would then guide the selection of rules and procedures. By putting this theory into practice, teachers understand that the role of rules is to develop expectations of good behavior, that following the rules through the practicing of procedures should lead to a better school climate for the students, as well as the teachers.

Developing rules and procedures will require building positive, cohesive relationships within the group. Joe Hester, in his book *Bridges: Building Relationships and Resolving Conflicts* (1995), cites the work of Adler and Rodman (1982) as an important tool in helping us understand the process of conflict resolution. (I have added additional comments in brackets.):

1   **Shared goals.** People draw closer when they share a similar purpose or when their goals can be mutually satisfied. [The group, led by a facilitator, must acknowledge the goals and the potential for meeting them.]

2   **Progress toward these goals.** While a group is making progress, members feel highly cohesive. [Make sure that the progress of the group is visible. Write down what is said. If a particular idea demands discussion, then discuss it, but all efforts must be focused on working toward a solution, not a debate.]

3   **Shared norms and values.** While successful groups will tolerate, and even thrive on, some differences in member attitudes and behaviors, wide variations in the group's definition of what actions or beliefs are proper will reduce cohesiveness. [The group must stay focused on what is being done and agree to work together. As mentioned above, difficult points can be discussed, but discussion shouldn't stop progress. Move on, and come back to sticky points later. Above all, seek consensus. (Consensus does not mean we all agree on everything, but that we will support the group's efforts and decisions.)]

4   **Lack of perceived threat between members.** A cohesive group is usually one in which members see no threat to their status, dignity, and material or emotional well-being. [Members are not there to blame others for previous failures. Sessions are not for pointing fingers, but for problem-solving.]

5 Interdependence of members. Groups become cohesive when their needs can be satisfied with the help of the other members. [By working together, each individual can achieve his or her goals. Individual growth occurs through connecting with other members of the group.]

The faculty needs to foster development of consistent practices for themselves and the students by following steps like these:

1 Determine the rules which will lead to a better school climate for the faculty and students. This should be limited to five general rules. This must be done before working on the procedures or practices. The forms at the end of this chapter will act as your guide through this process. It is preferable that each person work individually *(Form 1)*; then work in small groups to reach consensus *(Forms 2 and 3)*; and finally, try to reach a group consensus *(Form 4)*. Remember, every voice should be heard.

2 Once the rules have been determined and consensus reached, procedures for students to follow which engender good habits should be delineated. Once again, work individually *(Form 5)*, then in a small group *(Forms 6 and 7)*. Afterward, reach consensus as the entire group *(Forms 8 and 9)*.

3 Once you have reached consensus as a faculty, take the same process to the student body. Have the students walk through the exercise. This can be done in elementary classrooms, middle school advisories, or high school homerooms. When students reach consensus in their groups, it is time for representatives from each homeroom/advisory to meet at a central location, share their work and reach consensus. You may need to adjust this for the primary grades.

4 Next, take the two lists. Note the many similarities between the faculty and student lists. Compare and contrast the lists, using *Form 3*. At this point, a joint panel of teachers and students could be convened. Finalize the procedures needed for the staff and students, then post or share the procedures. Provide a list of consequences that can occur if students choose not to follow the rules or practice the procedures. Have the students and staff begin following the procedures.

5 Celebrate your success!

The process of building rules and procedures will take several months to complete. Parents will appreciate efforts to implement the project for their children. Include the parents by seeking additional input from them before issuing the final product. The community may like to participate in the endeavor as well.

The real test, though, begins when students start practicing these character-developing procedures and teachers model and seek consistency across all grade levels. We must recognize students who are developing the good practices and encourage those who are struggling. Above all, we must be consistent.

Formulating rules and procedures requires that participants use common sense. However, this does not mean that it is easy. (Sometimes, focusing on rules obscures the important role procedures have in the development of good children). Far too many schools have assumed that students either knew the procedures or would quickly learn them. Experience tells us that many children may know the rules, but still struggle to practice the correct procedures. There are times when a child honestly does not know what he did wrong. Procedures and their practice help minimize these occurrences. Procedures are the foundation of any character development program. Procedures make following rules understandable and possible.

REVIEW

1   Rules are expectations of student behavior. They should be developed with the understanding that, upon following rules by practicing procedures, students are developing good character traits. Remember, the character traits we want students to develop should guide our formation of rules and our development of procedures. Ask, "What procedures must students practice in order to develop the habits of good character?"

2   Procedures are important. They help students develop the practices needed to form the habits of good character.

3   The more consistent a classroom, school and school district are in developing and practicing procedures, the greater the chances for students to develop good character.

4   Consequences must be established and enforced. We must seek consensus on what must occur when a student chooses to disobey a rule or refuses to follow established procedures. We should work to insure our consequences are fair and enforceable.

5   Good rules and procedures are possible and will make the lives of educators and students much better. Ask yourself, "Do you want to continue the rest of your career working in your present environment under the same circumstances?" If you want to change and improve the environment of your school, you must begin somewhere. Rules and procedures, practiced to develop good habits in children, are the first step toward civility.

RULES & PROCEDURES

6

CHAPTER 6

FORMS

TOOLS FOR PLANNING AND IMPLEMENTING RULES AND PROCEDURES

FORM 1

Individual work page for General Rules

Brainstorm a list of General Rules. At this point just get your ideas down. You will combine and omit some in the next step.

Develop three to five General Rules you wish to share with your group.

1.

2.

3.

4.

5.

FORM 2

Small-group consensus form on General Rules

Share your General Rules with the small group. Each person's General Rule will be written down below. Do not duplicate the General Rules. Just put a check mark beside duplicate ones. You may need additional space.

List your General Rules from the small group.

1.

2.

3.

4.

5.

FORM 3

Small-group consensus on General Rules

Examine the small-group's General Rules from Form 2. Combine and delete until you can reach consensus on three to five General Rules. These will be shared with the total-group.

Group Consensus

List your three to five General Rules from the small-group consensus.

1.

2.

3.

4.

5.

FORM 4

Total-group consensus on General Rules

Examine the small-group's General Rules. Combine and delete until you can reach consensus on three to five General Rules.

Group Consensus

List your three to five General Rules from the total-group consensus.

1.

2.

3.

4.

5.

FORM 5

Individual work page on Procedures

Taking the total-group's three to five General Rules, write two to four Procedures or practices under each rule. This will be shared with the small group.

GENERAL RULE 1

Procedures

1.

2.

3.

4.

5.

GENERAL RULE 2 (FORM 5: Individual work page on Procedures)

. . . .

Procedures

1.
. . . .

. . . .

. . . .

2.
. . . .

. . . .

. . . .

3.
. . . .

. . . .

. . . .

4.
. . . .

. . . .

. . . .

5.
. . . .

. . . .

. . . .

GENERAL RULE 3 (FORM 5 Individual work page on Procedures)

. . . .

Procedures

1.
. . . .

. . . .

. . . .

2.
. . . .

. . . .

. . . .

3.
. . . .

. . . .

. . . .

4.
. . . .

. . . .

. . . .

5.
. . . .

. . . .

. . . .

GENERAL RULE 4 (FORM 5 Individual work page on Procedures)

. . . .

Procedures

1.

. . . .

. . . .

. . . .

2.

. . . .

. . . .

. . . .

3.

. . . .

. . . .

. . . .

4.

. . . .

. . . .

. . . .

5.

. . . .

. . . .

. . . .

. . . .

Procedures

1.
. . . .

. . . .

. . . .

2.
. . . .

. . . .

. . . .

3.
. . . .

. . . .

. . . .

4.
. . . .

. . . .

. . . .

5.
. . . .

. . . .

. . . .

FORM 6

Small-Group Work on Procedures

List the total group's three to five General Rules below. Now write Procedures under each rule with each member sharing his or her ideas. There is no need to duplicate the Procedures. If it has been said, just put a check beside it to denote agreement.

GENERAL RULE 1 (FORM 6: Small-group work on Procedures)

Procedures

1.

2.

3.

4.

5.

GENERAL RULE 2 <small>(FORM 6: Small-group work on Procedures)</small>

. . . .

Procedures

1.
. . . .

. . . .

. . . .

2.
. . . .

. . . .

. . . .

3.
. . . .

. . . .

. . . .

4.
. . . .

. . . .

. . . .

5.
. . . .

. . . .

. . . .

GENERAL RULE 3 (FORM 6: Small-group work on Procedures)

Procedures

1.

2.

3.

4.

5.

GENERAL RULE 4 (FORM 6: Small-group work on Procedures)

. . . .

Procedures

1.
. . . .

. . . .

. . . .

2.
. . . .

. . . .

. . . .

3.
. . . .

. . . .

. . . .

4.
. . . .

. . . .

. . . .

5.
. . . .

. . . .

. . . .

GENERAL RULE 5 (FORM 6: Small-group work on Procedures)

Procedures

1.

2.

3.

4.

5.

FORM 7

Final Small-Group Consensus on Rules and Procedures

Taken from the entire small-group list, reach consensus, and develop two to four Procedures or practices under each Rule. This will be the final small-group project.

GENERAL RULE 1 (FORM 7: Final Small-group Rules and Procedures)

Procedures

1.

2.

3.

4.

5.

GENERAL RULE **2** (FORM 7: Final Small-group Rules and Procedures)

Procedures

1.

2.

3.

4.

5.

GENERAL RULE **3** (FORM 7: Final Small-group Rules and Procedures)

· ·

Procedures

1.

2.

3.

4.

5.

GENERAL RULE 4 (FORM 7: Final Small-group Rules and Procedures)

. . . .

Procedures

1.
. . . .

. . . .

. . . .

2.
. . . .

. . . .

. . . .

3.
. . . .

. . . .

. . . .

4.
. . . .

. . . .

. . . .

5.
. . . .

. . . .

. . . .

GENERAL RULE 5   (FORM 7: Final Small-group Rules and Procedures)

. . . .

Procedures

1.
. . . .

. . . .

. . . .

2.
. . . .

. . . .

. . . .

3.
. . . .

. . . .

. . . .

4.
. . . .

. . . .

. . . .

5.
. . . .

. . . .

. . . .

FORM 8

Procedures from small-group to total group

List the General Rules below. Now write the Procedures under each Rule with each group sharing its ideas. There is no need to duplicate the Procedures. If the Procedure has been said, just put a check beside it to denote agreement.

GENERAL RULE **1** (FORM 8: Procedures from small-group to total-group)

Procedures

1.

2.

3.

4.

5

GENERAL RULE 2 (FORM 8: Procedures from small-group to total-group)

Procedures

1.

2.

3.

4.

5.

GENERAL RULE 3 (FORM 8: Procedures from small-group to total-group)

Procedures

1.

2.

3.

4.

5.

GENERAL RULE 4 (FORM 8: Procedures from small-group to total-group)

. . . .

Procedures

1.

2.

3.

4.

5.

GENERAL RULE 5 (FORM 8: Procedures from small-group to total-group)

Procedures

1.

2.

3.

4.

5.

FORM 9

Final Total-Group Rules and Procedures

Taken from the entire group list, reach consensus and develop your final two to four Procedures (practices) under each Rule. This will be the final group project. You will have your Rules and Procedures after this is completed.

GENERAL RULE **1** (FORM 9: Final Total-group Rules and Procedures)

Procedures

1.

2.

3.

4.

5.

GENERAL RULE **2** (FORM 9: Final total-group Rules and Procedures)

. . . .

Procedures

1.
. . . .

. . . .

. . . .

2.
. . . .

. . . .

. . . .

3.
. . . .

. . . .

. . . .

4.
. . . .

. . . .

. . . .

5.
. . . .

. . . .

. . . .

GENERAL RULE 3 (FORM 9: Final total-group Rules and Procedures)

. . . .

Procedures

1.

. . . .

. . . .

. . . .

2.

. . . .

. . . .

. . . .

3.

. . . .

. . . .

. . . .

4.

. . . .

. . . .

. . . .

5.

. . . .

. . . .

. . . .

GENERAL RULE 4 (FORM 9: Final total-group Rules and Procedures)

Procedures

1.

2.

3.

4.

5.

GENERAL RULE 5 (FORM 9: Final total-group Rules and Procedures)

Procedures

1.

2.

3.

4.

5.

CHAPTER 7

QUESTIONS
AND OPTIONS ON
RULES AND PROCEDURES
FOR EDUCATORS

My travel and work around the country with schools interested in character education has resulted in some wonderful discussions on the role of rules and procedures in schools. Following are some questions and answers that were offered by educators concerning rules and procedures. I hope their concerns and responses will be helpful to you in your efforts.

Question...

By making a standard set of rules and procedures for all teachers in a school, I relinquish the authority that I have, as a teacher, to make an individual decision concerning the enforcement of a rule, the practice of a procedure or the implementation of a consequence. Is this a valid concern?

Answer...

This is a realistic concern. Where does the authority of a teacher end and the need for consistency throughout a school begin? Various individuals have offered different slants on this issue. One primary teacher argued that it was impossible, and perhaps not desirable, for primary students to be completely quiet in the hall. She felt that requiring students to be silent in the hallway was wrong. Others in the group recognized her concern, but reminded her that students who talk loudly to other students in the hall disrupt others. Whispering can quickly become much louder and result in disruptions.

Secondly, some of the teachers felt that asking children not to talk in halls unless talked to by an adult was an important habit to develop in children as young as kindergartners. It may be difficult at first, but if all primary teachers are consistent, children can develop the habit of not talking in the hall—unless talked to by an adult.

Clearly, if for example, noise in the halls has not been a problem with teachers in the past in a school, then it should not be raised now. Rules are developed as expectations of appropriate student behavior. The rule is not needed if the students are already exhibiting good behavior. They already must know it or understand the expectations of civil behavior.

Question...

Getting highly structured in rules and procedures can interfere with what I value in the classroom. It doesn't bother me if students are a little late. If I haven't started class, then this is not a very big deal. Secondly, why should I feel that I should always agree with the school? These students are mine and I reserve the right of autonomy.

Answer...

What do we want our children to learn? Do we want them to learn to budget their time and be accountable for being punctual, or does it matter from teacher to teacher? Some may consider this a violation of the autonomy of the teacher, especially if the teacher teaches the same children all day with no other teachers involved.

However, this is not the norm. Even in elementary schools, students have multiple teachers. The need for consistency is crucial for helping students know what is expected of them in the regular classroom, as well as in P.E., art, music and other similar courses. This should not change from teacher to teacher. If so, it becomes too confusing for the students and results in loss of instructional time for the teacher.

Now, this does not mean that a teacher can't have some procedures or practices in the classroom which are different from those of other teachers. For instance, a teacher may want students to check math papers in a certain way, or have them turn their papers in after they have evaluated their own work according to a prescribed axiom. This is fine. However, all teachers must follow the rules and procedures that have been agreed upon by the others in the school, especially concerning basic civilities and students' movements in and around the school.

Question...

You feel that students can contribute to the establishment of rules and procedures. Isn't that the job of the teacher or the school?

Answer...

Students can contribute to the rules and procedures of a school. The establishment of rules and procedures is a job of teachers, but it is not theirs exclusively. Students know what contributes to a good environment. We hope they are committed to doing their part in creating a civil environment. Ask their input; they spend the day with you. Ultimately, it is the teacher's responsibility to insure a good, safe climate in the classroom, but students can help.

Question...

Character education seems to reflect the opposite of the self-esteem movement. Isn't it important that children feel good about themselves, and can't character education actually damage their self-esteem?

Answer...

It depends on how you define self-esteem. If you believe that it is based only on getting "my" needs met and "my" feelings respected, then character education or any climate that expects civility can hurt a child's self-esteem. *Feeling* good is not the same thing as *being* good. Self-esteem is earned through the development of positive traits and attributes that are shared with others.

Developing good habits that contribute to social and/or academic success will enable students to feel good about themselves. Self-esteem must be earned, It cannot be given away like stickers on a primary student's paper. Developing positive self-esteem requires that students and adults interact with caring and trust. Self-development demands that one seek the guidance, care, discipline and love of others.

Bibliography

Beck, Ken and Jim Clark (1985), *The Andy Griffith Show Book.* New York: St. Martin's Press.

Bennett, William. (1994), *The Index of Leading Cultural Indicators: Facts and Figures on the State of American Society.* New York: Simon and Schuster.

Damon, William. (1995), *Greater Expectations: Overcoming the Culture of Indulgence in our Homes and Schools.* New York: Free Press.

Goldman, David. (1995), *Emotional Intelligence.* New York: Bantam Books.

Gossen, Diane Chelsom. (1992), *Restitution: Restructuring School Discipline.* Chapel Hill, NC: New View.

Hester, Joe. (1995), *Bridges: Building Relationships and Resolving Conflicts* Chapel Hill, NC: New View.

Josephson Institute of Ethics. (1996), 1996 study of 6,000 high schools students. Marina Del Rey, CA: Josephson Institute of Ethics Publishing.

Kauffman, James and Harold Burbach (1997), On Creating a Climate of Classroom Civility. Phi Delta Kappan. Vol. 79, No. 4. (December) 320-325

Kelly, Richard (1981), *The Andy Griffith Show.* Winston-Salem, NC: John F. Blair Publishing.

Kilpatrick, William. (1992), *Why Johnny Can't Tell Right from Wrong.* New York: Simon and Schuster.

Leming, James. (1993), "In Search of Effective Character Education." *Educational Leadership,* Vol. 51, No. 3 (Nov.): 63-71.

Research and Development Center for Teacher Education at the University of Texas. (1981), *Organizing and Managing the Elementary School Classroom*. Austin, TX: School of Education.

Sweeney, Jim. (1988), *Tips for Improving School Climate*. Arlington, VA: American Association for School Administrators.

Wong, Harry and Rosemary Wong. (1991), *The First Days of School*. Sunnyvale, CA: Harry Wong Publications.

Wilson, James Q. (1993), *The Moral Sense*. New York. Free Press.

Wynne, Edward A., and Kevin Ryan. (1997), *Reclaiming our Schools: A Handbook on Teaching Character, Academics, and Discipline*. Merrill/ Prentice Hall.

The New World Dictionary of the American Language. Second College Edition, 1986.

About the Author

Dr. Philip Fitch Vincent brings more than 20 successful years of experience in education. With an academic background in philosophy, religion, and psychology, Dr. Vincent received his master's degree in education from Appalachian State University in 1979 and his doctor of education degree in curriculum and instruction from North Carolina State University in 1991.

He has taught at the elementary, middle, and high school levels in North Carolina and Alaska, and has taught education courses at North Carolina State University. He has been a director of middle-grades education in North Carolina's Catawba County school system.

Dr. Vincent has authored or co-authored 18 books, including *Philosophy for Young Thinkers* and the best selling books *Developing Character in Students—A Primer for Teachers, Parents & Communities*, and his *Promising Practices in Character Education—Nine Success Stories from Across the Country*. Among journal articles he has written are articles about developing character, gifted education, computer ethics, and working with at-risk students in an alternative classroom setting. He is a regular contributor to various educational publications.

Dr. Vincent makes keynote presentations and conducts workshops with schools and parents on a variety of educational topics. He has been a featured speaker at many national education conferences including the following: Association for Supervision and Curriculum Development

(ASCD), Virginia Superintendent's Conference, Kenan Ethics Program at Duke University, North Carolina Principal's Executive Program, N.C. Superintendent's Executive Program, St. Louis Personal Responsibility Education Process Conference, National School Board Association, Midwest Principal's Conference, Oregon Association of School Administrators, Louisiana Department of Instruction, Florida Character Education conference, South Carolina Character Education Conference, North Carolina Middle Schools Association, N.C. DARE Conference, Character Counts Coalition–Connecticut Conference, North Carolina Character Education Conference, Florida Thinking Skills conference; as well as lecturing at Charleston Southern University, Olivett College, Western Carolina University, among others.

In North Carolina, Dr. Vincent has worked with more than 33 school districts in formulating and implementing their character education programs as well as working with schools and school districts in 23 other States.

Among awards Dr. Vincent has received are a Teaching Merit Award, a grant from the Council for Basic Education, and Phi Kappa Phi and Phi Delta Kappa induction.

Book Title

Book Title	Quantity	Price	Total
TEACHING CHARACTER			
Teacher's Idea Book		$24.00	
Parent's Idea Book		$12.00	
CHARACTER ADVISOR/ADVISEE			
25 Short Lessons to Develop Character in Students		$24.95	
CHARACTER EDUCATION WORKBOOK			
A "How-To" Manual for School Boards, Administrators & Community Leaders		$12.00	
RULES AND PROCEDURES			
The First Step Toward School Civility		$14.00	
PROMISING PRACTICES IN CHARACTER EDUCATION			
Nine Success Stories from Across The Country		$12.00	
DEVELOPING CHARACTER IN STUDENTS			
A Primer for Teachers, Parents & Communities		$12.95	
LESSONS FROM THE ROCKING CHAIR			
Timeless Stories For Teaching Character		$12.00	
JOURNEYS IN EDUCATION LEADERSHIP			
Lessons From Eighteen Principals of the Year		$12.00	

Subtotal	
NC Tax (6%)	
Shipping Total	
Total	

SHIPPING:
Up to $25 .... $4
$25 to $100 .... $6
Over $100 .... 6%

Form of payment: Check ☐   PO # ☐

Make checks payable to:
Character Development Group, PO Box 9211, Chapel Hill, NC 27515-9211

Ship To:

Name

Organization _____ Title

Address

City: _____ State: ___ Zip:

Phone: ( ) _____ Signature:

FAX ORDERS: (919) 967-2139

For further information, or to schedule a Character Development Workshop, call **(919) 967-2110**, or e-mail to **Respect96@aol.com**

Visit our WebSite at **charactereducation.com**

(Call regarding quantity discounts) R&P98

CHARACTER DEVELOPMENT GROUP

PO Box 9211
Chapel Hill, NC 27515

CHARACTER DEVELOPMENT GROUP offers complete resources, including publications and staff development training for the planning, implementation and assessment of an effective character education program in schools and school systems.